The Lure of Lighthouses

The Lure of Lighthouses

*The Inspiring Journey of the Lights,
Keepers, Ghosts, Sea & Sentiment
Of Our Timeless Lands-End Sentinels*

By
Alan Ross

WALNUT GROVE PRESS
Nashville, TN 37211

ISBN 1-58334-045-9

In most instances, material for this book was obtained from secondary sources, primarily print media. While every effort was made to ensure the accuracy of these sources, the accuracy cannot be guaranteed. For additions, deletions, corrections or clarifications in future editions of this text, please write WALNUT GROVE PRESS.

Printed in the United States of America
Cover Design: *Bart Dawson*
Front Cover Photo of Portland Head Lighthouse: *Convention & Visitors Bureau of Greater Portland (ME)*
Back Cover Photo of Block Island Southeast Light: *Cindy Horovitz Wilson*
Typesetting & Page Layout: *Sue Gerdes*

1 2 3 4 5 6 7 8 9 10 • 99 00 01 02 03

ACKNOWLEDGMENTS
The author gratefully acknowledges the friendship, deep support, and opportunity extended by Dr. Criswell Freeman, whose dependable guidance is our own steadfast beacon of inspiration.

My continuing thanks to Karol, whose devotion to our love is as reassuring as the Cape Hatteras Light itself.

Special thanks also to the magnificent staff at Walnut Grove Press, whose tireless efforts make it all magically happen.

For Anna

Through the years, your caring furnishment of
love and light has encouraged me along my
favorite thoroughfare —
the old lighthouse road.

Other WALNUT GROVE PRESS Books by Alan Ross

A Brief History of Golf
Echoes from the Ball Park
Hooked on Hockey
Golf à la cart
Big Orange Wisdom
Wildcat Wisdom
Total Soccer

Non-Sports Titles

Love Is Forever (co-written with Karol Cooper)

Table of Contents

Remembrance

On a nearly full moonlit summer night long ago in the mid-1950s, I said my first hello to a lighthouse. It was also to be the occasion of my introduction to the old game of grunion-running.

The Graham and Ross families were vacationing on that magnificent northeast seaside hideaway, Block Island. One evening, some of the older children leaked the news that "the grunion are running tonight." As the youngest, I was soon filled with anxiety. Would I get to go along on this great adventure? Yes, came back the consensus vote.

Our destination was the old North Lighthouse. It had already long been retired from service, as swirls of four-wheel-drive tire marks attested to upon our arrival. Naturally, I was soon the gullible target of play by the water's edge.

"There's one!" "Oh, did you see that!?" "Alan, look, over here…oh, you just missed it!"

I never did see the grunion run, not that night or any other. But I treasure the still-vivid memory of the moonlight pursuit of that silver-sided ghost fish along the beaches beneath the dark apparition of the vacated lighthouse. Fortunately, "Old Granitesides" would not be forgotten by the island's residents, who would later take up its preservation and ensure its existence for future generations.

a.r.

Introduction

It's not every day that you get to meet James Cagney at one of the great lighthouses in America.

I was a 12-year-old in the backseat of my parents' car, on a sunny afternoon in Nantucket, in the summer of 1956, when the famed Hollywood actor leaned into the driver's side window and said hello, before setting a date to go painting with my father, artist Alex Ross. Straight ahead through the windshield, past the silver-red of Cagney's hair, was the highly identifiable red-and-white-striped tower of the Sankaty Head Lighthouse. It all added up to a major mental photo op.

In researching the fascinating topic of lighthouses for this book, the subject's vastness became quickly apparent. Prolific are the works penned by countless qualified authors over the years — Snow, McCormick, Holland, Witney, Gibbs, De Wire, Jones, and so many others who have walked the lighthouse road before me. I tip my cap to them and their meticulous tomes, which document the voluminous history of our great aids to maritime navigation. Also, a word of commendation to the dedicated people helping to preserve these great structures from time and erosion.

To the majestic beacons. May they forever burn bright.

The lighthouse — any lighthouse,
whether huddled on a hilltop or perched
precariously on rocks miles offshore — is a
monument to the evolution of tribal primitive
to civilized man.

Dudley Witney
author

The history of lighthouses is the story
of a continual search for the best type of light
for use in aids to navigation.

Dennis L. Noble
author

Chapter 1

Origins: The First Lighthouses

The ancient sources speak many times about the lighthouse itself, but they don't give many details on this building, they give only an impression. They say that it was impressive for the Greek people and, after them, for the Romans and even for the Arabs.

Jean-Yves Empereur
French archaeologist,
at the rescue excavation site
of the ancient Pharos of Alexandria lighthouse,
1997

The First Lighthouse

It is generally believed by a consensus of historic accounts that the very first lighthouse was the famed Pharos of Alexandria, built around 300 B.C. by Egyptians on the island of Pharos, located at the head of the harbor to the port of Alexandria. It took 20 years to complete and was a colossal structure measuring over 500 feet in height. Reportedly, it was in service for an unimaginable 10 centuries and, though later inactive, remained structurally intact for an additional 500 years before toppling from an earthquake. Atop the phenomenon, one of the original Seven Wonders of the Ancient World, burned a wood fire or torches, the world's initial light source, as well as its most primitive one.

Columbus Had Lighthouse Ties

Little is recorded about lighthouses through the Dark Ages, but the Italians led the way in lighthouse development during the mid-12th century with a light erected on the island of Meloria in 1157. Genoa came next in 1161, and a structure with a tower was built near Leghorn in 1163. Other lights — at Venice, Tino, and one near the Straits of Messina — would follow. With commerce beginning to open up between European countries, England and France soon completed lighthouses as well.

It is said that the lighthouse at Genoa, which lasted well into the 15th century, stirred the passion of a young Christopher Columbus for the sea. His uncle, Antonio Colombo, was its keeper in 1449 and the only family member not in the weaving trade.

Until early in the 20th century, the Cordouan
lighthouse was considered the finest
in the world, and some say it still is.

Dudley Witney

Too little is known of this reverend personage,
this martyr of the Seas. It is, I believe, the most
venerable of all the European lighthouses…
Cordouan stands on a reef which is never dry.
Great, indeed, was the audacity which
ventured to raise it in the midst of the waves,
in the violent flood, in the everlasting battle
between such a river and such a sea…
An eternal warfare is waged against it.

Jules Michelet
author (1875)

Cordouan — A Lighthouse Castle for the Ages

In 1584, The Ritz-Carlton of lighthouses, the posh Cordouan light at the mouth of the River Gironde, which funnels into France's Bay of Biscay, was begun under the direction of Louis de Foix on a commission from Henri III. The light, while a landmark for architectural grandeur and sumptuous living, still functioned as a serviceable lighthouse.

The structure took 27 years to build and featured keepers' quarters in the lower section measuring 134 feet in diameter and a spacious central hall 52 feet wide. On the second floor was a chapel, a most unusual accoutrement for a lighthouse. The upper floor, 197 feet above the sea, contained a huge lantern and chimney for wood fire use. The spiral staircase off to one side enabled the utilitarian chores of fire maintenance to be conducted without disruption of the main rooms. The exterior was a marvel of columns, ornate windows, statues and frescoes.

The sea ultimately threatened de Foix's magnificent project, when the island began to wash away from the relentless pounding of waves. De Foix then built a barrier around his work of art and finally lit a fire of oak atop the unique structure for the first time in 1611.

Eddystone Light – Part I

It took three tries, beginning in 1696, but the English were finally able to secure a fabled lighthouse at the treacherous Eddystone Rocks, 14 miles off the port of Plymouth in southern England. In one of the more bizarre stories about lighthouse construction, the original Eddystone work crew was *hijacked* by a French privateer in 1697 and smuggled off to France, where they remained in custody until exchanged for French prisoners of war. A year later they were back at the light, laboring to finish Eddystone builder Henry Winstanley's 80-foot wooden tower. A more detailed account of the plight of the Eddystone Light is described in chapter two's Great Wave-Washed Lighthouses (pg. 31).

Lighting the Way

The story of the actual lights within the lighthouses is a tale of constant refinement of man's earliest light source — the flame.

Wood fires on hilltops segued into wood fires at the tops of towers. In the early New England colonies, lighted baskets hanging from poles were placed on the tops of hills as early navigational aids to local vessels. Not until the 16th century was another form of fuel, slower-burning coal, introduced. Candles also illuminated the lights and were less messy than wood or coal, though not as bright.

In 1781, Frenchman Ami Argand invented a lamp that had a hollow circular wick and a parabolic reflector. It issued a smokeless light equal to seven candles and used half as much oil as the spider lamp — the incumbent method of illumination at the time. Argand's lamp and reflector became the standard for lighthouses around the world...except in America.

The U.S. Lighthouse Road

In 1789, just 13 years after America claimed her independence, Congress voted to empower the U.S. Treasury Department with jurisdiction over all aids to navigation, lighthouses included, in the United States.

Thirty-one years later, in 1820, the number of lighthouses in the United States had grown from 12 to 55. But that same year signaled the beginning of the notorious run of the fifth auditor of the Treasury as general superintendent of lighthouses. The 32-year period that followed, under the penny-pinching scrutiny of Stephen Pleasonton, has been deemed the low point in American lighthouse history.

Under Pleasonton, some glaring irregularities took place. For instance, a naval officer appointed to investigate Pleasonton found that between two standard locations along Maine's coastline there were *nine* lights. At Nauset, on Cape Cod, *three* lighthouses were built only 150 feet apart from each other, when it was evident that one would have more than done the job (see page 143).

Politics Slow America's Pace

*One wonders how many ships that
wrecked during Pleasonton's 32-year
administration would have been saved
had more effective lights been available.*
                    — *F. Ross Holland, Jr.*

A man little versed in maritime affairs, Stephen
Pleasonton depended heavily upon the advice of
contractors with nautical knowledge and experience.

One of these suppliers, an unemployed ship captain named Winslow Lewis, developed his own ver-
sion of the Argand lamp in 1812. Though Lewis' light
was an improvement over the previous lamp of
choice, the spider lamp, it was inferior to Argand's
model. Pleasonton, known more for his fiscal talents
than his wisdom of navigation aids, bought Lewis'
sales job hook, line, and sinker. In addition,
Pleasonton's agreement to have all the country's
lighthouses refitted with Lewis' invention shut the
door on America's opportunity to procure the
vaunted Fresnel lens, a prism lens so magnificent
that it is still in use in many lighthouses today.

Pleasonton's blatant display of favoritism would
set back U.S. lighthouse development 40 years.

The Fresnel Lens

French physicist Augustin Fresnel's revolutionary lens, developed in 1822, quickly became *de rigueur* among lighthouse lighting mechanisms worldwide, everywhere that is but the United States.

The beehive-looking Fresnel (pronounced freh-nell) lens surrounded one single lamp. Prisms of glass at the top and bottom refracted, or bent, the light; together with the powerful magnifying glass in the middle of the lens a narrow, strong, concentrated beam of light was created — the most powerful light source ever devised up to that point.

Fresnel broke down his gradation of lenses by degrees, from First Order (the strongest, used for major seacoast lights) down to Sixth Order (usually utilized as harbor or channel lights).

Eventually, after Congress voted in 1852 to install a new Lighthouse Board to replace the Treasury Department's fifth auditor as head of lighthouses, America caught up with the rest of the world, ordering Fresnel lenses from France for all its existing lighthouses. Before the start of the Civil War, every U.S. lighthouse had been fitted with a Fresnel.

Moving Ahead

The nine-member Lighthouse Board that replaced the disastrous Pleasonton reign in 1852 is credited with making vast headway in the escalation of U.S. lighthouse development and with placing America on a par with the rest of the world's competency of service. In 1910, Congress undertook a move to streamline the country's aids-to-navigation operation by voting to institute the Bureau of Lighthouses, appointing one man in charge and cutting back military involvement in lighthouse service. Finally, in 1939, the U.S. Coast Guard adopted all U.S. lighthouses and is the official custodian of most to this day.

Early Presidents Involved with Lighthouses

Early American presidents George Washington, John Adams, Thomas Jefferson and well-known statesman and this country's first secretary of the treasury, Alexander Hamilton, all had actual hands-on experience governing the nation's lighthouse matters.

Because America was young and the affairs of running the United States weren't as voluminous as they are today, presidents could take an active role in approving individual lighthouse construction projects, as well as okaying the appointment and dismissal of keepers. But it wasn't long before a quickly emerging America made it impossible for the chief officer to personally oversee navigational concerns. It then was delegated to the domain of the secretary of the treasury.

It vibrated and trembled with every shock of the wind and sea....The lighthouse shakes at least two feet each way. I feel as seasick as ever I did on board a ship.

Visitor to the original
Minot's Ledge Lighthouse
in March 1851,
one month before a severe storm
tumbled the structure into the sea,
killing two assistant keepers.

Chapter 2

The Great Wave-Washed Lighthouses

My father was the keeper
            of the Eddystone light,
And he slept with a mermaid one fine night.
       From this union there came three,
A porpoise, a porgy, and the other was me.

Old sailor's folk song

The Eddystone Light — Part II

The first of the great wave-washed lighthouses, the Eddystone, 14 miles off the southern coast of England, is considered the world's most famous 17th-century lighthouse.

Originally erected by Henry Winstanley in 1698, the stone-based, wooden polygonal structure was a marvel for its apparent soundness atop a brutally hostile location. Twelve-foot long iron rods encased in a stone base were anchored to the Eddystone Rocks but weren't strong enough to withstand a tumultuous storm on November 26, 1703, which left no trace of the tower, Winstanley, or his work crew and keepers.

The next lighthouse at the demonic site, a building of similar construction to the original that was supervised by John Lovett and John Rudyerd, was finished in 1708 and stood for 47 years before being gutted by a fire.

The light's third edition was engineered by John Smeaton, who, in 1759, constructed a tapered conical tower made entirely of stone that stood for well over a century, before being reassembled, stone by stone, near Plymouth, England, in 1982.

It caused the loss of 70 sail of vessels
in a storm which happened upon the coast
in the month of December 1799.

Committee of the House of Commons Report
on the notorious Bell Rock

The Bell Rock is most dangerously situated,
lying in a track which is annually navigated
by no less than 700,000 tons of shipping.
Its place is not easily ascertained.

Committee of the House of Commons Report
circa 1803-1805

Bell Rock

A deadly reef lying on the northern side of Scotland's Firth of Forth, Bell Rock (also called Inchcape Rock) became the target of the Northern Lighthouse Board and Scottish engineer Robert Stevenson in the early 1800s after continuously taking its toll on area shipping boats.

Following the path of John Smeaton's success with the Eddystone Light a half century before, Stevenson anchored a rugged double layer of bolted stone deep within a 42-foot pit excavated into the rock that served as the light's foundation. A tapered tower was erected above the site, and lanterns encased within red glass gave the beacon a distinctive look. On February 1, 1811, after five years of patient, solid assembly, the Bell Rock Light was lit.

The significance of its construction, along with that of the Eddystone Light, was that engineering and technological advances had now made it possible for lighthouses to be erected on even the most lethal of natural settings.

An interesting piece of Bell Rock lore surrounds the origin of its name. The Abbott of Aberbrothock, from the monastery in Arbroath, on the mainland 11 miles from Inchcape Rock, once affixed a bell to a float on the hazardous reef. It was tolled by the natural action of the sea and alerted mariners to the danger lurking there.

The Great Wave-Washed Lighthouses

Courtesy of U.S. Coast Guard

Minot's Ledge

The North American equivalent of the Eddystone and Bell Rock lights is Minot's Ledge, a man-made wonder lying in often tumultuous seas on the Cohasset Rocks, 20 miles southeast of Boston.

The first tower constructed on the 25-foot ledge lasted just 16 months before a savage storm toppled it, taking two assistant lighthouse keepers down with it (see the quote fronting this chapter). Though built on steel legs imbedded in rock, it was clear the structure was no match for nature's fury.

For the second tower, huge stones totaling 2,367 tons were cut to interlock with each other then layered in two tiers to form the impregnable forty-foot high foundation of the lighthouse. It was engineered in such a way that the relentless surf would only make the granite stones grip tighter. Finally in 1860, amidst great celebration, the light was lit.

One holds a certain awe of this fortress when it is learned that gargantuan 100-foot waves have periodically rolled over its top. The legendary tower, considered the Lighthouse Board's single greatest achievement, still stands to this day.

Sometimes I think the time is not far distant when I shall climb these lighthouse stairs no more. It has always seemed to me that the light was part of myself....Many nights I have watched the lights my part of the night, and then could not sleep the rest of the night, thinking nervously what might happen should the light go out....I wonder if the care of the lighthouse will follow my soul after it has left this worn out body!

Abbie Burgess
legendary lighthouse heroine and onetime
assistant keeper at desolate Matinicus Rock, Maine

Chapter 3

Keepers of the Light

Few actual lighthouses supported the generally mistaken impression that keepers led the ultimate romantic life by the sea, with ample time to pursue artistic and leisurely pursuits.

Summer tourists and visitors usually took home sentimental images of a pristine panorama of beauty under optimal weather conditions. They weren't around to view firsthand the struggle for existence that surrounded scenic but remote wilderness settings like the famed Split Rock Lighthouse on Lake Superior, where serious isolation prevailed during winter, from mid-December to early April, when lake traffic was suspended, as well as in the years before Minnesota's North Shore highway was built, in 1924.

And not many civilians were privy to seeing a keeper wrap a rope around his waist as a precaution against railing winds and waters, while en route to the tower or fogbell from his quarters, at a dreary and dangerous offshore site like Mount Desert Rock in Maine.

Though the mind's lingering recollection of lighthouses will always lean slightly to the romantic, the reality of a keeper's life was anything but a whimsical, carefree, poet's dream.

Lighthouse Suite in B♭ Minor

A former keeper of the barren Mount Desert Rock Lighthouse off the coast of Maine, was fond of surprising his wife with gifts upon his return, as the tale goes, from periodic visits to the mainland for supplies. The lonely, often-treacherous trek required negotiating the 23 miles of sea that separated the Rock from the mainland in a dory rowed alone by the keeper. It wasn't uncommon for a trip to last several weeks, depending on the disposition of the weather.

Usually the keeper returned from Southwest Harbor with presents along the lines of planting soil, flower seeds, a jar of cloves, a roll of yellow oilpaper, and the like. But on one occasion, the keeper's wife noticed that two men sat in the dory as it approached the Mount Desert Rock landing. The keeper had brought back an elderly man carrying a tuning fork and a set of rachets.

Only two hours were needed for the man to tune the missus' salt-and-sea saturated old piano.

He wound up with a prolonged stay on the Rock, however. Ten days of inclement weather delayed his departure.

A lighthouse is no place for a fat man.
Space is at a minimum!

Henry Goshorn

I notice how the monotony of a quiet life
stimulates the creative mind.
Certain callings…entail such an isolated life.
I think of such occupations as the service
in the lighthouses.

Albert Einstein

All rising to great place is by winding stair.

Francis Bacon

Painting the Tower

Coating the lighthouses with paint was an arduous ritual for the keepers. A ladder usually took care of the bottom part of the tower, but often only some kind of jerry-rigged scaffolding or barrel lowered from the catwalk by ropes could get at the upper reaches.

In addition, for the safety of mariners during daylight hours, many of the towers were painted with distinctive design patterns as daymarks to differentiate themselves from other beacons. That meant additional hardships for lighthouse painting.

For instance, upkeep on the monstrous barber shop pole-like Cape Hatteras Light regularly took its toll on dozens of paint brushes while consuming hundreds of gallons of paint.

We had no electricity and we had
no refrigeration; we had no communication
with land, so we had to use our own ingenuity.
At times, it would be so rough you couldn't
get over to shore for at least six to 15 days.
I had to make my own bedding, I had to make
my own clothes, I had to knit us socks and
mittens...everything about the house
I had to make and do by hand.

Connie Small
wife of keeper Elson Small,
Lubec Channel, Avery Rock, Seguin Island, St. Croix lights

If you were on a northshore station and
something went wrong, you couldn't very well
call a plumber or an electrician. You had to
either do it yourself or do without.

Frank Schubert
last U.S. civilian lightkeeper,
Coney Island Light (NY)

Keeper's Help Elevates Wright Brothers

The famous Wright Brothers, Orville and Wilbur, got a boost from a lighthouse keeper and his wife for their very first attempt at lofting a flying machine back in the early 1900s.

The Wrights' first experimental glider, in fact, was built in the front yard of Currituck Beach Lighthouse keeper W.J. Tate. The two brothers were hosted by Tate and his wife during their time in Kitty Hawk, North Carolina. Tate often assisted the Wrights, loaning them tools and support as needed, while his wife cooked meals to nourish the men and lift their spirits.

It was Mrs. Tate, operator of the local post office, who first received contact from Wilbur Wright. The Ohio inventor had inquired by letter, in 1900, about the weather and topographical conditions in the Kitty Hawk area to determine its suitability as a potential site for the brothers' historic work, which eventually culminated in the successful launch at Kill Devil Hills in 1903.

The Light-Keeper

As the steady lenses circle
With frosty gleam of glass;
And the clear bell chimes,
And the oil brims over the lip of the burner,
Quiet and still at his desk,
The lonely Light-Keeper
Holds his vigil.

…This is his country's guardian,
The outmost sentry of peace,
This is the man
Who gives up what is lovely in living
For the means to live.

Poetry cunningly guilds
The life of the Light-Keeper,
Held on high in the blackness
In the burning kernal of night,
The seaman sees and blesses him,
The Poet, deep in a sonnet,
Numbers his inky fingers
Fitly to praise him.
Only we behold him,
Sitting, patient and stolid,
Martyr to a salary.

— *Robert Louis Stevenson*

I knew no other life, so I was sort of fitted
for it. I never had much of a childhood,
as other children have it. That is, I never knew
playmates. Mine were the chickens, ducks
and lambs, and my two Newfoundland dogs.

Kate Moore
who spent 72 years at Black Rock Lighthouse,
Bridgeport, CT
(1806-1878)

It would be almost a miracle if today a family
would be content to be in such a lonely spot,
even though the TV and radio gave them
contact with the outside world. Contentment
in family life is nonexistent as compared with
that of years gone by. The restless age,
in which we are trying to exist, would be
incomprehensible to those of the age
in which they (light keepers) lived.

Mrs. E. Williams
Dartmouth Free Press,
October 13, 1971

Another day of vacancy, another day
of disrepair. It really doesn't take long for the
paint to start peeling off the walls and the
ceiling, for the wood to start pulling up and
the nails to start coming through.
It really goes downhill fast.

Daniel McLean
Coast Guard keeper

Everybody's sorry to see keepers go...
it leaves the whole question of what happens
to the lighthouses hanging.

Sarah Gleason
Rhode Island Parks Association

A new era of keepers is emerging —
the caretakers.

Susan Sulavik Peters

It was a good life. It was a lonesome life, but I thanked God every day for it.

Mrs. Marie Carr
keeper's wife,
Little Gull Light and Block Island Southeast Light

I ain't particularly strong. The Lord Almighty gives it to me when I need it, that's all.

Ida Lewis
legendary lighthouse heroine

Chapter 4

Courage and Dedication

The Flying Santa

In 1927, Captain Bill Wincapaw became disoriented flying on a stormy December night while trying to return to a Maine airfield. Suddenly, through the dark foggy blanket, the aviator recognized the Dice Head Lighthouse beam and, with his sense of direction restored, made it down safely to the ground. In appreciation, Wincapaw dropped a package of goods to the lighthouse keeper and his family from his plane the day before Christmas. It occurred to Wincapaw that Christmastime would be the perfect occasion to salute other unsung, valiant keepers of the light elsewhere along the coast. But it is lighthouse historian and author Edward Rowe Snow who became most popularly associated with the role of the Flying Santa.

For almost 50 years Snow faithfully dropped gifts from the sky for lighthouse families every holiday season except 1942, when he was with the air corps in North Africa. Snow's Santa sorties were executed in cycles, with 40 lighthouses making his regular rotation. By 1955, Snow was sky-dropping his yuletide bundles to a staggering 250 lighthouses annually, including one remarkable run in which gifts were dropped at Fire Island Light off the Long Island shore and California's Point Vicente Lighthouse in the same day — in a prop plane, remember.

A typical Flying Santa gift package included gum, cigarettes, candy, cigars, balloons, rubber balls, dolls, pocket-edition books, Gillette razor blades, picture puzzles, and the latest volume of a Snow-authored book.

On Maine's Cape Porpoise Light, keeper Joseph Bakken's family would erect their Christmas tree and adorn it with lights, then wait for the drop from the Flying Santa before decorating the tree with the contents of Snow's package.

Then there was the famous "bombing" of Ipswich Light in Massachusetts. Snow, who fashioned an exemplary 91 percent accuracy rate with his air-drops, hit his target perfectly — perhaps just a bit too perfectly. With the keeper's family anxiously awaiting the imminent arrival of the airborne St. Nick, what to their wondering ears should appear but Snow's gift-missile hurtling through the cottage skylight, eventually coming to rest in the upper hallway of the house. A miniature sleigh and eight tiny reindeer could not have trashed the place more.

Intimidating Minot's Ledge Light proved to be Snow's most testing trial. Having to land his package on the virtual head of a pin, Snow's otherwise impressive delivery-drop stats took a dive at the Ledge — converting just 40 percent, while the surrounding sea made off with the goods a majority of the time.

Stag Stations

Some lighthouse outposts were so remote and forsaken that it was determined by the Lighthouse Service, in the latter part of the 19th century, that no men with wives and children could be assigned to them. Only single men (or married men willing to live apart from their families) qualified for duty at these solitary beacons called stag stations.

Usually these locations were offshore rock lighthouses. Interestingly, island lighthouses were deemed suitable for families, though often they were as desolate as the rock lights.

Among the better-known stag lights were: St. George Reef (California), Tillamook Rock (Oregon), Mount Desert Rock (Maine), Saddleback Ledge (Maine), Spectacle Reef (Lake Huron), Scotch Cap (Aleutian Islands, Alaska), Stannard Rock (Lake Superior), Minot's Ledge (Massachusetts), Cape Sarichef (Aleutian Islands, Alaska) and Cape St. Elias (Alaska).

Could You Take It?
Three Years On, One Year Off

A keeper assigned to one of the planet's remote outposts, like the Scotch Cap and Cape Sarichef light stations in the Aleutian Islands way out on the western keys of Alaska, had an unfathomably tough life. So tough that even boats delivering mail and supplies to these lonesome destinations sometimes could not land near them in bad weather. Normal leave time was not a realistic possibility at such distant sites. Therefore the keepers' work/leave schedule usually called for one year off for every three years of active service.

A June 1915 notice in the *Lighthouse Service Bulletin* made mention of purchasing "line-throwing guns" to aid in landing mail and other necessary provisions, including even the transport of the keepers themselves, to and from shore at these world's end locations.

"I Can Depend on You, Abbie"

No discussion of desolate outposts is complete without mention of Maine's Matinicus Rock, and no mention of the Rock is complete without recollecting Abbie Burgess.

Abbie, the daughter of Matinicus Rock Light keeper Samuel Burgess, moved to the Rock when she was 14. Steadily gaining familiarity with the lighthouse chores, Abbie got an unwanted baptism under fire during a brutal January storm in 1856.

Her father, forced to make a vital trip to Rockland 25 miles away for family provisions, left Abbie, now 17, in charge of running the light and taking care of her invalid mother and three sisters. By midday of the same day of Samuel Burgess' departure, an ugly storm was forming out of the northeast.

For three days the gale raged. On the morning of the fourth day, Abbie moved her mother and younger sisters to a safer building on the Rock. It would later prove to be critical.

Realizing that they could all perish with no food, Abbie then made a heralded dash to the hen house and scooped up all the hens, except one, just before a giant wave washed the coop away. The timing of her rescue was crucial. As she hastily fastened the door behind her, hens in hand, her little sister standing by a window exclaimed,

"Oh, look! Look there! The worst sea is coming!" That wave obliterated the old stone dwelling her mother had earlier been moved from. The timing of the hen rescue was strategic too, for it would be four long weeks before the weather let up enough for Samuel Burgess to return. When he finally did make it back he found the exhausted family had subsisted mostly on eggs and corn meal mush for nearly a month.

But what turned Abbie's nightmarish experience into historic legend was the fact that not once did she fail to light the lamps in the Matinicus Rock towers during the entire time of her father's absence. Word of her heroism quickly spread.

Abbie would later marry the son of the man who succeeded her father as keeper of Matinicus Rock. Not long after the two were wed, she received her own official appointment as assistant keeper at the Rock, a position she had faithfully tended for so many years in an unofficial capacity.

In 1875, Abbie's husband received his own appointment to tend the White Head Light, approximately 20 miles inland from Matinicus. They both served that station until 1890, when Abbie's failing health forced their retirement.

The ocean's voice never receded for the woman whose reliability was once so depended upon by others. During her time at Matinicus Rock, Abbie wrote, "The sea is never still, and when agitated, its roar shuts out every other sound."

With its great sweeping arm extending more than seventy miles out into the Atlantic, Cape Cod is one of the most formidable navigational obstacles on the planet. Over the centuries, more than three thousand vessels have come to grief on the Cape's coarse glacial sands. No one knows how many seamen have perished...

Ray Jones
John Grant
authors, Legendary Lighthouses

Chapter 5

Dire Straits

Rattlers Rattle Keepers

You'd think a lighthouse would be the safest place in the world from snakes, but reptiles often sought its safety in storms and active high tides. In addition, they often were indigenous to the land immediately surrounding the lighthouse, as was the case with the Matagorda Light in Texas, where both rattlesnakes and water moccasins were prevalent.

Many a keeper's log noted confrontations with snakes. In December of 1912, the assistant keeper of the Wadmelaw River Light in South Carolina noted a terrific buzzing noise above his head as he ascended the final steps to the tower. Seeing a giant rattlesnake wrapped around the light box itself, the man armed himself with an oar and somehow managed to sling the creature overboard with his thrusts into the water far below. But the angered snake, instead of swimming away, headed back to the beacon and proceeded to begin curling up the steps *again*! The scene, incredibly, was virtually repeated, complete with a second oar bashing by the assistant keeper, before the persistent rattler finally accepted defeat.

Unaware that they stood on the brink of eternity, the crew of the Fitzgerald shared the bond that has always made brothers of sailors, and, for that matter, of lighthouse keepers. They were men caught in the grip of a hostile sea.

Ray Jones

The Wreck of the *Edmund Fitzgerald*

Few disasters at sea ever received more fame than the sudden and shocking disappearance of the world's onetime largest freighter, the729-foot-long *Edmund Fitzgerald*, on November 10, 1975, on turbulent Lake Superior. The event is forever etched in history and folklore, thanks to Canadian singer/songwriter Gordon Lightfoot's mega-million-selling hit record of 1976 that brought the grim catastrophe worldwide attention.

What was so stunning about the incident was its modern-day occurrence, something that didn't enter the realistic realm of possibility in the age of advanced navigational technology. After all, we'd already put men on the moon.

But happen it did, with a fury and havoc that still leaves its followers mystified. Loaded with 26,013 tons of milled iron ore, "Big Fitz," as her crew of 29 called her, headed downlake out of Duluth on a clear day. But increasing gale force winds reached 70 miles per hour by midday, while waves rolled like terrifying 30-foot serpents.

Attempting to make Whitefish Point at the southeast end of the mammoth lake, the *Edmund Fitzgerald* received no help from the usually reliable Whitefish Point Lighthouse, a victim of the raging storm itself. For one of the few times in its 128-year history, the sentinel was dark, due to power failure from the storm.

A trailing ship, the *Arthur M. Anderson*, suddenly lost track of the *Fitzgerald* on its radar. After alerting the Coast Guard, a massive search ensued. The *Edmund Fitzgerald* had vanished into thin air.

Not until a joint team of marine scientists in 1989 sent a Remote Operated Vehicle down to robotically investigate the silent grave of the *Fitzgerald* did the truth behind the freighter's quick demise finally surface.

Many theories were voiced in the immediate aftermath of the calamity, but the probing cameras of the research effort proved that the great ship had plummeted 500 feet, bow first, to the chilling darkness of Lake Superior's floor. The previous reigning popular belief held that the massive hull had split in two on the surface, perhaps balancing momentarily between two giant waves under both the bow and stern before snapping in half from the weight of the cargo of ore.

November brings a marrow-deep chill to the bones of sailors on the Great Lakes. It's not just that the weather gets colder but also that the lakes themselves take on a different character. They turn tempestuous and develop sharp, unpredictable tempers. Storms can blacken their faces in a matter of minutes and churn their waters into a confusion of towering waves capable of breaking a ship in half....Tired sailors pushing themselves and their ships to the limit make a habit of looking back over their shoulders. They are watching for November — not the one on the calendar but the one that comes calling when you least expect it. Among Great Lakes sailors it is sometimes said that "Thanksgiving comes only if you survive November."

Ray Jones
author

The Great Lakes Hurricane of 1913

Many storms on many seas have claimed many lives over the centuries. But rarely have disparate elements teamed to create such incredible havoc as the brutal assault of three major storm fronts that collided head on over the Great Lakes in early November of 1913.

Emanating from three different directions, the trio of fronts created what virtually amounted to an inland hurricane. From the Rockies came a system carrying water that first gained weight far out in the South Pacific. Out of the Caribbean came a typhoon-like front, and finally, from the Bering Sea, came freezing rains.

They hit with the fury of a three-headed Medusa.

For nearly five days the maelstrom raged unabated. When the skies mercifully cleared, over 40 ships had gone down. With them went 235 sailors and passengers.

Lake Huron took the full brunt of the storm. Dozens of ships were devoured by the Thunder Lake, with no less than eight massive freighters disappearing without a trace, à la the *Edmund Fitzgerald*. Taking the plunge to their watery graves were 178 seamen and passengers aboard the fateful eight.

Every 50 years these great gales come, the waves dashing clear over the island, and on Jan. 19, 1820, the last of the old trees on Fayerweather Island was swept away.
The lighthouse itself blew over once when I was there (Sept. 22, 1821). It was a dreadful thing to have happen, for this was then the only light on the Connecticut side of Long Island — the only light between New Haven and Eaton Neck — and was of course of inestimable value to mariners. Sometimes there were more than 200 sailing vessels in here at night, and some nights there were as many as three or four wrecks, so you can judge how essential it was that they should see our light.

Kate Moore
keeper,
Black Rock Light,
Bridgeport, CT
(1871-1878)

Scotch Cap and the 1946 Tsunami

It was no April Fool's Day joke.

What happened at the Scotch Cap Lighthouse on desolate Unimak Island in the Aleutian Islands, on April 1, 1946, will not long be forgotten in sea lore.

The light was situated on a concrete pad halfway up a cliff side, 92 feet above sea level. But from out of a clear, calm, starlit night would come a horror of unimaginable proportions.

At 1:30 AM, the stillness was suddenly shattered by an earthquake tremor from the Pacific, lasting 30 seconds, that rattled the lighthouse and all of Unimak Island. A second tremor reverberated 27 minutes later. Unbeknownst at the time, just 18 minutes away, a titanic tidal wave with the stealth of a panther was powering its way toward land.

Like the volume on a stereo that's slowly increased came the sound of a hundred aircraft approaching the cliff. Outlined against the sky was a giant tsunami that dwarfed the lighthouse. Cresting high overhead, the thunderous sea in a flash swallowed the Scotch Cap Light whole, like Jaws in a feeding frenzy. Seismologists estimate the wave's height at over 100 feet.

The light was leveled. Only the concrete pad survived. Five keepers' lives were lost and, though a new lighthouse was built 500 feet above the sea, it came too late for the doomed men of Scotch Cap.

Had it not been for the prompt assistance of A.A. Howard...it would have ended seriously....I was taken from the bottom of my dory and carried to the lighthouse where I was furnished with dry clothing and made as comfortable as possible.

Walter C. Harding
on his rescue by Stage Harbor Light (MA) keeper
Alfred A. Howard, circa 1907-1914

Chapter 6

Rescue!

See Spot Run

In the 1930s, at Maine's Owls Head Lighthouse, which fronts the gateway to Rockland Harbor, a springer spaniel named Spot carved his name into local folklore with his uncanny canine abilities.

The most well-known story involving Spot's rescuing skills centers around a raging blizzard on a night in which the Matinicus mailboat operator's wife, Mrs. Stuart Ames, called Owls Head keeper Augustus Hamor to see whether her husband's boat had been spotted in the storm. The keeper replied he could not even see the water from the tower, so poor was the visibility. The woman then asked if the keeper's dog, who never missed a chance to welcome the mailboat back to port, could be let outside to see if he detected the missing vessel anywhere.

Spot was quickly dispatched but returned cold and wet, curling up in a shiver by the warm fire in the keeper's quarters. Suddenly, he sprang to the door to be let out again. Spot bounded through the snow to the fog station, grabbing the fog bell rope in his teeth but to no avail — the bell was frozen solid. Next the dog went scurrying down the rocky path to the beach and began barking furiously.

Not long after, three toots from the invisible boat signaled that its captain had heard Spot's call and was proceeding to the channel back to safe harbor.

The Hamors reportedly buried Spot below the fog station.

I have come to see Ida Lewis, and to see her
I'd get wet up to my armpits if necessary.

Ulysses S. Grant
18th president of the United States,
on getting his feet wet while landing at Lime Rock Light,
1869

Miss Lewis, I want to smoke
on your half-acre rock for half an hour.

Admiral George Dewey

General William Tecumseh Sherman sat out
on the rock for nearly an hour, asking me
questions about my life, and saying he was
glad to get to such a peaceful place.

Ida Lewis

Ida did things that women usually didn't do
in her day. She pulled up her skirts,
got into a boat, and rowed to the rescue.

Elinor De Wire

Sometimes the spray dashes against these
windows so thick I can't see out...but I am
happy. There's a peace on this rock
that you don't get on shore.

Ida Lewis

Ida Lewis – America's Queen of Rescue

If ever the lighthouse service yielded a bonafide star from its ranks, it was the legendary heroine Ida Lewis, whose rescue efforts became fascinating story matter for several national magazines and elevated her to the level of an idolized celebrity.

Born the daughter of cutter captain Hosea Lewis, who was appointed keeper at Rhode Island's Lime Rock Light in 1854, Ida could outrow any boy her age as a youth. At age 16, she made her first rescue, saving four young boys from drowning who had capsized their sailboat near Lime Rock.

Eight years later, in 1866, she saved the life of a drunken soldier attempting to take a shortcut over water to nearby Ft. Adams with two of his friends. The rollicking trio had noticed Ida's brother's skiff on the shore and lit out in the small craft for the fort. Inexplicably one of the men, in his inebriated stupor, began to kick at a plank in the bottom of the boat and soon sank the skiff. Ida quickly responded, jumping to her lifeboat and reaching the man still clinging to the sides of the overturned skiff. The near-dead weight of the soldier posed recovery problems for Ida, who injured herself in the rescue and needed almost a year to fully heal. His two companions swam toward shore, but it is not known if they ever made it.

Ida's exploits became the subject of a cover-story piece for *Harper's Weekly*, the leading publication of the era. Other stories appeared in *Leslie's* and *The New York Times*. Her sudden exalted status attracted the likes of President Ulysses S. Grant, Admiral George Dewey, General William Tecumseh Sherman, and "every Mrs. Astor and every Mrs. Vanderbilt and every Mrs. Belmont you ever heard of." All made personal visits to Lime Rock Light to meet the famed heroine.

One of Ida's most unusual efforts involved the rescue of a sheep. On a cold January morning in 1867, three men herding one of August Belmont's prize sheep through the streets of Newport saw the animal suddenly break for the wharf and unaccountably plunge into the icy water. The men spotted Ida's brother's new skiff (oh no, not again!) on the beach near Jones' Bridge and set out after the unfortunate sheep, who by this time was quickly drifting away. In their desperation in the choppy water, it wasn't long before the little craft capsized, and Ida was off to another rescue. She first rowed to the three men and, after hauling each aboard, deposited them all safely on shore. Next she headed out for the little lost sheep, which by now was almost a speck on the horizon. An hour later, though, Ida and the sheep returned to the extremely grateful men.

Though she faithfully served almost all her entire life at Lime Rock Light, Ida was officially appointed its head keeper in 1879 and held that post until her death, at age 69, in 1911. She is credited with saving the lives of 23 people.

Rescued Dog Was Warm Spot in Keeper's Heart

In 1883, life was good for Kate Walker. Newly married, she lived with her husband, John, at the northern New Jersey seaside tower of Sandy Hook, where he was keeper.

But within two years they were transferred to Robbins Reef, the barren sparkplug lighthouse on the west side of the gateway channel to New York Harbor. Kate was so depressed by her new isolated surroundings that she initially refused to unpack. But she stayed, and when her husband suddenly died from pneumonia less than a year later, Kate began her long 33-year tenure at the desolate light.

She is credited with over 50 rescues, but none gained her more fame than the little Scotty dog she pulled out of New York Harbor when a three-masted schooner the pet was on went down. All but given up for dead, the little dog was revived by Kate and soon became a welcome addition to life at Robbins Reef Light. However, several weeks after the disaster, the dog's master, fully recovered from the harrowing ordeal of the shipwreck, returned for his canine pal.

It was a tearful but heartfelt farewell that day for Kate and her two children. Later, she would say that of the many people she had rescued over the years few were as appreciative as the wet little dog she had lifted out of the harbor on the tip of her oar.

The Frozen Lovers of Owls Head

Shortly before Christmas, in 1850, a man engaged to be married brought his bride-to-be back to his cabin on board a small schooner anchored in Rockland Harbor. A lone deckhand remained on the ship with them.

That night a brutal storm severed the schooner's anchor cables and set the ship adrift. Murderous winds whipped them into jagged rocks near Owls Head Light at the far end of the harbor.

Their only chance for survival was to huddle under blankets and let the freezing spray from the waves form an ice shell over their bodies.

In the morning, the deckhand somehow managed to free his arms and furiously picked at his frozen tomb with a knife, eventually freeing himself. He gave up his companions for dead.

Setting out for Owls Head Lighthouse, the deckhand barely made it to the keeper's cottage. After being revived, he led an expedition back to the schooner with little hope that the man and woman would still be alive. What the rescue party saw on arrival stunned them: a couple locked in a lovers' embrace inside a cocoon of frozen ice a foot thick.

The men extricated the bodies and took them to the lighthouse. Two hours later, the girl stirred; an hour after that the man awoke from his frozen sleep. They were later married that coming June.

The lighthouse and lightship appeal to the interests and better instinct of man because they are symbolic of never-ceasing watchfulness, of steadfast endurance in every exposure, of widespread helpfulness. The building and the keeping of the lights is a picturesque and humanitarian work of the nation.

George R. Putnam
first commissioner of lighthouses (1910-1935),
Bureau of Lighthouses

Chapter 7

Safety of the Sentinels

Guidance of the Guardians

Lighthouses are like anchors.

> *David Candee*
> *bosun's mate first class,*
> *U.S. Coast Guard*

Lighthouses speak to vigilance.
They speak to caring.
They speak to being there.
They speak to helping
other human beings.

> *Peter Ralston*
> *the Island Institute,*
> *Rockland, Maine*

The sunset is behind a bank of dark clouds,
yet it is not gloomy for the poets and
our good sense teaches us there is
a Silver Lining beyond.

> *Keeper's logbook*
> *Calumet Harbor Entrance Lighthouse,*
> *Lake Michigan,*
> *November 13, 1880*

For every one of us there is an appeal
in these isolated sentinels, suggesting hope
and trust. Standing alone on the ocean
highways, they represent the eternal
watchfulness of their keepers, whose slogan
through the ages has been vigilance.

Edward Rowe Snow
lighthouse historian/author

Lighthouses are not just romantic,
lonely sentinels against a dark and evil sea.
They're symbols of hope — and defiance.

Wayne C. Wheeler,
president,
U.S. Lighthouse Society

So tonight wandering sailors pale with fears
Wide o'er the watery waste a light appears,
Which on the far-seen mountain blazing high
Streams from lonely watchtower to the sky.

Homer

Excerpts from
"The Lighthouse"

The rocky ledge runs far into the sea,
And on its outer point, some miles away,
The lighthouse lifts its massive masonry,
A pillar of fire by night, of cloud by day.

Even at this distance I can see the tides,
Upheaving, break unheard along its base,
A speechless wrath, that rises and subsides
In the white tip and tremor of the face.

And as the evening darkens, lo! how bright,
Through the deep purple of the twilight air,
Beams forth the sudden radiance of its light,
With strange, unearthly splendor in the glare!

Like the great giant Christopher it stands
Upon the brink of the tempestuous wave,
Wading far out among the rocks and sands,
The night o'er taken mariner to save.

They come forth from the darkness, and their
sails Gleam for a moment only in the blaze,
And eager faces, as the light unveils
Gaze at the tower, and vanish while they gaze.

The mariner remembers when a child,
On his first voyage, he saw it fade and sink
And when returning from adventures wild,
He saw it rise again o'er ocean's brink.

Steadfast, serene, immovable, the same,
Year after year, through all the silent night
Burns on forevermore that quenchless flame,
Shines on that inextinguishable light!

The startled waves leap over it; the storm
Smites it with all the scourges of the rain,
And steadily against its solid form
Press the great shoulders of the hurricane.

The sea-bird wheeling round it, with the din
Of wings and winds and solitary cries,
Blinded and maddened by the light within,
Dashes himself against the glare, and dies.

A new Prometheus, chained upon the rock,
Still grasping in his hand the fire of love,
It does not hear the cry, nor heed the shock,
But hails the mariner with words of love.

— *Henry Wadsworth Longfellow*

A Merry Minot's Christmas

So much has been written about the dangers, legends, and ghostlore at dreadful Minot's Ledge Light, off the Massachusetts coastline. But another frightening incident recorded in the light's logbook is worth mentioning.

The Christmas storm of 1909 surely gave new meaning to the term "wave-washed lighthouse" to Minot's Ledge keeper Milton Reamy, who watched in stunned astonishment as a gargantuan 170-foot wave crested high over the tower. The solitary beacon has unsettlingly felt many a giant breaker shake its granite walls in facing some of the world's highest waves during its tenure on the Cohasset Rocks.

We have all kinds of navigational equipment
— satellites, Lorans, depth sounders,
compasses — all these wonderful things.
But when your eye sees that lighthouse
at night, that red sector or that white sector,
you know where you are.

Rick Amory
president,
Virginia Pilots Association

Home is where you've got to get back to,
and...the lighthouse is kind
of a good thing to see.

David Candee

I have learned to depend on (the Cape Henry
Lighthouse) as I think every mariner that
comes in and out of here depends on it.
Lighthouses have been around a long time.
They are literally a beacon in the night.
They are a comfort, a security blanket.

Rick Amory

Safety of the Sentinels

My dad taught us to turn the light on...
But it was just a job to us and a home.
I never thought about what it was doing
for the ships. It was just our life.

Sarah Owens Schwartz
one of six daughters of
former keeper William Owens,
Point Arena Lighthouse, California

The light was like a baby.
You tended it like a baby because people's lives
depended on it.

Connie Small

Living at a lighthouse is an education...
Coming home to the lighthouse is coming home.

Susan Lessard
town manager, Vinalhaven, ME,
and resident of Brown's Head Light

It was like being Tom Sawyer
I had the roam of sixty-eight acres surrounded
by water and half a mile of shore.

Tom Skolfield
who grew up at Maine's Seguin Island Light

When we were on the light, we didn't think of it as a job. We thought of it as a calling.

Connie Small

Lighthouse keepers,
like cowboys and pirates,
continue to fascinate us
though their time
has passed.

Robert Sheina
former Coast Guard historian

Chapter 8

Romance and Sentiment

There is so much you think that isn't needful to say.

Kate Walker
legendary Robbins Reef Lighthouse keeper

You will find the lighthouse keeper playing
at the piano, making ship models and bows
and arrows, studying dawn and sunrise
in amateur painting, and with a dozen other
elegant pursuits and interests to surprise
his brave, old-country rival.

Robert Louis Stevenson

The lighthouse was thought to be a tonic
for the body and the soul.

Elinor De Wire

I've never met anyone who didn't like
a lighthouse or a caboose.

Charlotte Johnson
director,
Rose Island (RI) Lighthouse Foundation

Lighthouses represent something
people really can't touch.

Bill Thompson
Friends of Nubble Light preservation group

A lot of people who come here are looking for a warm, friendly beacon. It's not only the beauty, it's the sound, the smell, the light.

Greg O'Brien
author/producer of films about Cape Cod

Cape Cod seems built for lighthouses.... Long ago it put to sea and has been underway ever since.

Admont G. Clark
author

The lighthouse is a connection to the past. If you lose the past, you lose Cape Cod.

Greg O'Brien

If we added up all the tanks of gas, phone calls,
and odds and ends we have brought down here,
the price would be prohibitive. But a little bit
at a time doesn't seem to hurt so bad.
To spend the night here and watch the sunset
is worth an awful lot of work.

Jim Walker
preservationist,
Race Point Lighthouse, Cape Cod (MA)

It's a wonderful place to come on a beautiful
afternoon and sit and watch the ocean.

Thomas Laverty
historic preservation specialist,
on New Jersey's Navesink Lights

In these sizzling hot days I know
of no excursion so pleasant as a jaunt
to the Light House.

Joshua Freeman
keeper, Portland Head Light (1820-1840)

Lighthouses are intriguing
because they're a part of
a frontier that we haven't
conquered yet. The sea
is the last frontier
here on earth.

Elinor De Wire

The lighthouse has some sort of magical, universal appeal. People will come from anywhere in the country just to be able to stay in a lighthouse.

Jeffrey Burke
owner,
Isle Au Haut Inn (ME)

In the minds of summer tourists, the life of the keeper was all sunshine and gentle breezes, wildflowers peeking up from fissures in the rocks, fish jumping, and picnics spread on the green lawn.

Elinor De Wire

It was prestigious. It was prestigious to the level of legend. It was a time when the song, the romance of the sea would lavish itself upon this kind of person (light keeper). These were the Americans who stood out. And they, of course, in an idealized way, typified the Romantic era.

Brian Sullivan
executive director,
The Newportant Foundation

You don't realize the importance
of (the lighthouse) or the beauty of it until
you get older and move away from it.

Diana Owens Brown
one of six daughters of
former Point Arena (CA) Lighthouse keeper
William Owens

When I look back on it, I'd say we had a very
good life. I wish we could get back to it.

Shirlee Owens Storms
daughter of former Point Arena (CA) Lighthouse keeper
William Owens

Unfortunately, the job of a lightkeeper
has boiled down to nothing much more
romantic than a caretaker.

Daniel McLean
Coast Guard keeper

We had a wonderful life. We would play games at night, and when the Coast Guard boys would stop by, they'd have a cup of coffee or something — always a piece of cake or a piece of pie. One of the Coast Guard boys said, "Oh, Mrs. Carr, I could smell your pie and cake way out to sea." Oh, gosh, when I think of it, what a happy life that was. I think it broke my husband's heart when he had to leave Block Island. He never was the same.

Mrs. Marie Carr

Nothing moves the imagination like a lighthouse.

Samuel Adams Drake

Chapter 9

Haunted Lighthouses

UFAU

Eighteen miles distant from the legendary isolated Au Sable Lighthouse, on the extreme northern Michigan wilderness of Lake Superior, the lighthouse tender *Amaranth* was witness to an unsettling yet awesome light apparition on the night of August 21, 1930.

A beam of light, estimated by the ship's captain and crew to be approximately 100 feet wide and located directly above the tender, appeared for over an hour before mysteriously and suddenly vanishing. It was ascertained that the light was not the beam from any lighthouse, nor was it a display on the part of the northern lights.

A report of the UFO-like ghost light was filed with Lighthouse Service officials in Detroit, but its origin was never determined and the light was never seen again.

Hardly a lighthouse exists that does not have some supernatural being associated with it.

Elinor De Wire

If you've seen one lighthouse ghost, you've seen them all.

Kenneth Black
retired Coast Guard officer

Jenny One Note

It wasn't always music to the ears of "Maineland" residents living near the mouth of the Kennebec River in the middle 1850s. For when the wind was just right, the resonance of a piano solo wafting out from the Seguin Lighthouse meant the music of lonely despair.

The keeper's wife, a frail woman who once charmed fellow churchgoers and friends on the mainland with her music, succumbed to boredom at the hands of lighthouse living and, eventually, to mental malaise. To buoy his failing wife, the keeper bought her a piano and ferried it out from the mainland. Along with the instrument, came one piece of sheet music. Over and over the one song was played, to the insane distraction of the keeper.

One night the familiar melody ceased as an unusual silence fell over the waters about the Seguin Lighthouse.

The mad keeper had strangled his wife, then demolished the piano with an axe.

The next lighthouse keeper at Seguin journaled about the fine fishing, seabirds, fog, etc., before noting the occasional sound of a piano somewhere playing a recurring haunting refrain.

Psychic Team Peers
Into Point Lookout Light

In 1987, a team of researchers from the Maryland Committee for Psychic Research, headed by Dr. Hans Holtzer, renowned for his work at the infamous haunted house in Amityville, began an investigation into the phenomena long recorded at the Point Lookout Light, a Chesapeake Bay area beacon which guided traffic in and out of the Potomac River until 1965.

The lighthouse's ghostly inhabitants include the spirit of Ann Davis, the wife of Point Lookout's first keeper and a keeper herself at the light for 30 years after her husband's death. Her sighs and voice, taped on the tower stairway, exclaimed that the lighthouse is "my home."

Rangers from nearby Point Lookout State Park have observed Joseph Haney's ghost, an apparition that peers into the back door of the lighthouse as storms approach. It is thought to be seeking refuge. Haney, a second officer aboard the steamer *Express*, drowned in an 1878 storm, and his body was found washed up on the shore near Point Lookout.

Holtzer's crew noted that numerous other spirits haunt the lighthouse as well, some no doubt from the nearly 4,000 bodies of soldiers buried there. During the Civil War, Point Lookout was the site of both a hospital and a prison camp.

Execution Rocks

Guiding mariners to the entrance of New York harbor from Long Island via the East River is notorious Execution Rocks.

Legend has it that the light got its name from the horrifying executions that took place there during the time of the American Revolution. American revolutionaries, chained by the British to the rocks at low tide, awaited a grisly death by drowning as the incoming tide returned.

But the ghosts of those pitiable souls may have gained a measure of sweet revenge. While pursuing George Washington's retreating army, a ship loaded with British soldiers was waylaid onto Execution Rocks, some say pulled in by the restless spirits themselves, and all aboard were drowned.

Fairport Wraith Not from Pet Cemetery

If displaced spirits do truly roam the earth in search of never-reached destinations, lost lovers, or missing body parts, it would be only reasonable to assume that pets have their ghostly equivalents too.

Though hardly a chapter from Stephen King's *Pet Cemetery*, Ohio's Fairport Lighthouse, on southern Lake Erie, reportedly houses a little spectral gray cat, who playfully darts from room to room in now-you-see-me-now-you-don't fashion. The light was converted into a maritime museum sometime after closing down as a navigational aid in 1925.

In 1989, museum curator Pamela Brent, who lived on the second floor of the old keeper's quarters, detected a wisp-like apparition that resembled a small puff of smoke. The little wraith turned out to be a playful kitten spirit, who on occasion would pounce upon a balled-up sock that Brent tossed to it.

Upon investigation, Brent discovered that the wife of 1870's keeper Joseph Babcock had taken ill for a lengthy period after the death of their young son. The playful antics of a little kitten apparently helped assuage the woman's grief. Interestingly, the cat would bound after, and retrieve, a small soft ball thrown by the woman from her bed.

Minot's Ledge Disaster

Barely more than a year after its much bally-hooed construction in 1850, off the terrifying Cohasset Rocks in Massachusetts, a storm of massive proportions rocked the original iron-legged screw-pile lighthouse at Minot's Ledge and plummeted the structure into the sea, taking down the two assistant keepers with it.

Keepers of the new Minot's Ledge Light, constructed in 1860, would hear tapping from time to time on the stovepipe within the lighthouse, like two men signaling each other. It was later found that the two deceased assistants communicated in that way while on different floors inside the old tower.

Passing mariners often noted the appearance of a tattered man hanging from the lower rungs of the tower ladder, waving as if to ward off vessels venturing too close to the perilous rocks during northeast storms. Foreign sailors said the forlorn figure was shouting "Keep away! Keep away!" in Portuguese, the native language of Joseph Antoine, one of the assistants who perished in the 1851 gale.

Minot's Ledge

Like spectral hounds across the sky
The white clouds scud before the storm,
And naked in the howling night
The red-eyed lighthouse lifts its form.

The waves with slippery fingers clutch
The massive tower, and climb and fall,
And, muttering, growl with baffled rage
Their curses on the sturdy wall.

Up in the lonely tower he sits,
The keeper of the crimson light —
Silent and awestruck does he hear
The imprecations of the night.

The white spray beats against the panes
Like some wet ghost that down the air
Is hunted by a troop of fiends,
And seeks a shelter any where.

Fitz James O'Brien
excerpted from "Minot's Ledge",
Harper's New Monthly Magazine,
April 1861

Penfield's Ghost of Christmas Past

Connecticut's Penfield Reef Light boasts several strange otherworldly tales.

On Christmas Eve 1916, light keeper Fred Jordan, just beginning his leave for the holidays, drowned in a severe storm while attempting to reach shore in a small boat. Later, when his body was found, the contents from one of his pockets revealed a note indicating an entry he had intended to make into the light station's logbook. Succeeding keepers at Penfield Reef indicated the presence of a spirit dressed in white that usually departed a room wherein the log was kept. The journal was opened to the page dated 24 December, 1916.

Another incident near the light involved a stricken powerboat that was guided to safety by a man in a rowboat who then suddenly disappeared.

A third story relates the rescue of two boys whose boat had capsized near Penfield Reef. A man dragged the two to safety, depositing them at the base of the light, before heading into the lighthouse itself. When the boys had caught their breath, they walked up to the beacon to personally thank their rescuer. He was nowhere to be found. The lighthouse was empty.

Heceta Head's Gray Lady

High atop a stretch of Oregon coastline, the Heceta Head Lighthouse is home to an elderly vision of gray — a woman who seems to be searching for something with a look of imploring need.

Strange but relatively benign occurrences, such as lost tools mysteriously reappearing or cupboards closed at night that were found open the following morning, gave a hint of hauntedness to Heceta.

In the 1970s, a workman cleaning windows in the keeper's quarters' attic came face to face with an elderly silver-haired lady who seemed terribly distressed. Coaxed back later to finish his job, the man accidentally pushed in one of the attic window panes from the outside. He obstinately refused to go inside and clean up the broken glass. That night the couple living in the old keeper's house heard scraping sounds above their bedroom ceiling. In the morning, they found that the broken glass in the attic had been neatly swept up.

Some years later, people playing the Ouija Board at the house inquired of the ghost's name. "Rue" was the reply. She is believed to be the mother of a small child that died tragically at the light long ago and whose grave for many years was carefully tended on the lighthouse grounds.

You never enjoy
the world aright,
Till the sea itself floweth
in your veins...

Thomas Traherne
Centuries of Meditations

Chapter 10

The Sea Has Its Say

Darkness settles on roofs and walls,
But the sea, the sea in darkness calls;
The little waves, with their soft, white hands
Efface the footprints in the sands,
And the tide rises, the tide falls.

Henry Wadsworth Longfellow
The Tide Rises, The Tide Falls

He who commands the sea
Has command of everything.

Themistocles
Cicero

Some sailors' tales have roots so deep in marine tradition they reach all the way back to the time of the Roman grain ships and before that to the age of Ulysses. The poetic memories of mariners are as ageless as the dangers they face.

Ray Jones

The seaman's story is of tempest...

Sextus Aurelius Propertius

Impetuously rages the Channel, through the narrow defile which ingulfs the rushing waters of the North. Violent is the Sea of Brittany in the boiling eddies of its basaltic recesses.

Jules Michelet

The widow-making unchilding unfathering deeps.

Gerard Manley Hopkins
The Wreck of the Deutschland

...the murderous innocence of the sea.

William Butler Yeats

A man who is not afraid
of the sea will soon
be drownded for he will
be going out on a day
he shouldn't. But we do
be afraid of the sea, and
we do only be drownded
now and again.

John Millington Synge
The Aran Islands

Roll on, thou deep and dark-blue ocean, roll!
Ten thousand fleets sweep over thee in vain;
Man marks the earth with ruin — his control
Stops with the shore — upon the watery plain
The wrecks are all thy deed.

Byron

The weltering flood
Of the huge sea, whose tumbling hills, as they
Turn restless sides about, are black or gray,
Or green, or glittering with a golden flame.

William Morris
The Earthly Paradise

The dragon-green, the luminous, the dark,
the serpent-haunted sea.

James Elroy Flecker
The Gates of Damascus

Every day the sea is carving up the shoreline,
and you can go down to Truro or Provincetown
or Wellfleet and see a different beach every day.

Greg O'Brien
author, film producer

My bounty is as boundless as the sea.

William Shakespeare
Romeo & Juliet

Water, water everywhere,
Nor any drop to drink.

Samuel Taylor Coleridge
The Ancient Mariner

Break, break, break,
On thy cold gray stones, O Sea!
And I would that my tongue could utter
The thoughts that arise in me.

Alfred, Lord Tennyson
Break, Break, Break

Anythin' for a quiet life, as the man said
wen he took the sitivation at the lighthouse.

Charles Dickens
Oliver Twist

We are as near to heaven by sea as by land!

Sir Humphrey Gilbert

Since once I sat upon a promontory,
    And heard a mermaid on a dolphin's back,
Uttering such dulcet and harmonious breath,
    That the rude sea grew civil at her song,
And certain stars shot madly from their spheres,
    To hear the sea-maid's music.

William Shakespeare
A Midsummer Night's Dream

If I take the wings of the morning,
    And dwell in the uttermost parts of the sea;
        Even there shall thy hand lead me,
        And thy right hand shall hold me.

Psalms 139:7-10

I do not know beneath what sky
        Nor on what seas shall be thy fate:
        I only know it shall be high,
        I only know it shall be great.

Richard Hovey
Unmanifest Destiny

Once more upon the waters, yet once more!
And the waves bound beneath me as a steed
That knows his rider!

Byron

But seas do laugh,
Show white,
When rocks are near.

John Webster

O we can wait no longer
We too take ship O soul,
Joyous we too launch out on trackless seas,
Fearless for unknown shores.

Walt Whitman
Passage to India

Paint me the bold anfractuous rocks
Faced by the snarled and yelping seas.

T.S. Eliot

I still seem to see his wan
countenance as he looked
out upon the Ocean
and exclaimed,
"It makes me tremble!"

Jules Michelet

And there it was in the sunlight of a winter morning, a high knuckle of rock on the out-thrust fist of Newfoundland, for centuries the first sight of land on the long wet way from Europe to Canada, and the last point of departure for sailors dead-reckoning on the voyage east. "There's Cape Race!" the gruff old skipper shouted. "Take a good look — you may never again see it this close." There on the cliff stood the lighthouse which had saved countless people from blind disaster, and beside it the insignificant-looking wireless telegraph shack that picked up the SOS of a stricken *Titanic*. Like many others of its kind, the lighthouse on Cape Race said two things to the mariner, "Keep off!" and at the same time, "Now you know exactly where you are."

Thomas H. Raddall

Chapter 11

Unforgettable Lighthouses

What goes into an unforgettable lighthouse? A dash of nostalgia, for sure. Perhaps a pinch of something you can't put your finger on but is always calming and comfortably reassuring.

Maybe it was a boyhood trip with the family to Block Island or Nantucket; perhaps a photo expedition to the Florida Gulf and intimate encounters with the lights at Old Port Boca Grande, St. Marks, Crooked River, Cape San Blas and, over on the Atlantic side, the Cape Florida, Ponce Inlet and Jupiter Inlet lights. Sometimes unforgettable things jump out at you from a book, poem, or painting. For sheer awe, I don't think I've ever seen anything to equal Lake Superior's Split Rock Light, and I've only seen pictures of it.

My list certainly would include the Pharos of Alexandria, magnificent Cordouan, the timeless Eddystone Light and fearsome Minot's Ledge, but since we've already addressed those legends I'm excluding them here.

A hundred different people would create a hundred different lists of favorite lighthouses.

Here's mine.

Portland Head Light

It is America's most photographed lighthouse and one of its most visited. Powerfully positioned on a promontory at the gateway to Portland Harbor, it staggers the artistic senses with its quaint clapboard/shingle-sided keeper's house, white split-rail fencing, classic white conical tower, and sweeping vista of the 365 islands in Casco Bay. Its view is said to be unrivaled along the entire Atlantic Coast.

Portland Head has inspired scores of poets and painters, among them Henry Wadsworth Longfellow and artist Edward Hopper, both of whom captured in their work the feel of coastal maritime life as frequent visitors to Portland Head.

For almost 60 years, the respected and admired Strout family maintained the famed light. Joshua Strout spearheaded a Christmas Eve rescue in 1886, when he and his crew saved all 18 people aboard the *Annie C. Maguire*. Subsequently it was found that the ship was on the sheriff's list for failing its creditors. Authorities had not expected the schooner to wash up virtually at their feet.

Portland Head, Maine's oldest light, is one of four now standing that was authorized by George Washington himself. Two cannonballs frame the lighthouse doorway, symbolizing the Colonial period in which the light was built (1791). The 80-foot tower stands 101 feet above high tide.

Courtesy of Convention & Visitors
Bureau of Greater Portland

The Maine lobster may adorn the state's license plate and place mats from Eastport to Kittery, but there is no more potent emblem of the rockbound coast and Maine's near-spiritual ties to the sea than the lighthouse.

Christopher Corbett
The Washington Post,
August 1, 1993

Portland Head Light is one of Maine's most famous landmarks, appearing on promotional brochures, postcards, sweatshirts, and even the label of Portland lager. After the L.L. Bean catalogue outlet and Acadia National Park, it's probably the third most visited spot in Maine.

Christopher Corbett

Courtesy of U.S. Coast Guard

Point Reyes Light

> *The sirens had been in operation for 176 consecutive hours and jaded attendants looked as if they had been on a protracted spree.*
>
> — *San Francisco Chronicle*
> *September 25, 1887*

Considered the West's most dangerous navigational obstruction, Point Reyes is a wicked jag of pitted rocky headland sticking 15 miles out into the Pacific, fairly taunting ships en route to San Francisco to either move...or else.

Ensconced almost 300 feet above the ocean on a craggy perch, the smallish lighthouse is entombed in fog an average of 110 days out of the year, and reportedly more than one keeper has lost his sanity over the relentless repetition of the fog signal.

A daunting 308-step incline stairway that leads up from the lighthouse to the keeper's quarters troubled keepers no end when weather was bad, which was just about all the time.

The building of Point Reyes Light was a construction nightmare, with the rough terrain posing an infinite number of logistical problems from simply transporting materials to blasting rock on the treacherous inclines.

Courtesy of U.S. Coast Guard

Cape Hatteras Light

Our august symbol of maritime majesty, the fabled Cape Hatteras Light (1803), reigning supreme on North Carolina's Outer Banks, boasts 193 feet in elevation as America's tallest lighthouse.

The mighty sentinel, with its distinctive black-and-white barber-pole stripes, stands watch over the most dreaded stretch of sea real estate on the Atlantic Seaboard — the infamous Diamond Shoals, a.k.a. "The Graveyard of the Atlantic." The deadly barrier, which extends almost 15 miles seaward, is the tempestuous meeting point of the cold northern Labrador Current and powerful southerly Gulf Stream. As you might expect, an oceanic imbroglio occurs when north meets south.

The legendary light marks Poseidon's favorite cemetery. Over 2,300 recorded wrecks of vessels over the centuries lie buried off Hatteras.

Erosion has been the Achilles' heel of the mighty tower, with the tireless Atlantic lapping to within 120 feet of the Hatteras base. But in the summer of 1999 the National Park Service moved the light 2,900 feet inland. Spokesman Bob Woody says the $9.7 million relocation effort should beat back the watery beast for another 100 years.

Courtesy of U.S. Coast Guard

Split Rock Light

There may not be a more picturesque lighthouse in America than the 38-foot octagonal Third Order light just north of Duluth, Minnesota, that perches stunningly 178 feet above Lake Superior "on a cloven precipice of brindled gray-brown rock," as poetically imparted by renowned lighthouse author Elinor De Wire.

Teeming with visitors in the summer months, Split Rock's breathtaking vistas are a magnet for picnickers and sightseers. The photogenic site also has been the source of creative inspiration for many artists and writers, including renowned American painter Edward Hopper and authoresses Daphne DuMaurier and Eugenia Price.

The need for the light was generated by unusual conditions: Large iron ore deposits in the area created magnetic interference, wreaking havoc with navigators' compasses. That problem was also compounded by the number of vessels carrying ore as cargo. In addition, foggy weather as well as extremely deep waters close to the rocky shore ultimately made it imperative that a light be built.

In 1910, sitting on just over seven and a half acres purchased by the government for $200, the grand light was first lit. It is no longer in service.

Courtesy of U.S. Coast Guard

Sankaty Head Light (Nantucket)

> *The narrow aperture in the platform*
> *under the lantern…has been widened to*
> *allow ladies with hoop skirts to pass up*
> *through to see the reflectors.*
> — *Nantucket Mirror*
> *October 25, 1856,*
> *on the Sankaty Head Lighthouse*

You've got to love a lighthouse where you once met actor James Cagney and whose nearby golf course of the same name is possibly America's only links golf course.

Built in 1850, Sankaty Head Light was the second lighthouse in the United States to have a cutting-edge Fresnel lens, also installed in 1850. Its second-order beam reportedly was bright enough to bait a hook.

A golf course of singular uniqueness adjoins the light. In his *To the Linksland*, author Michael Bamburger says, "Sankaty Head is not immediately on the sea, but it is duney and sand-soiled, windswept, treeless, and natural." Essential ingredients for a bonafide, Scotland-like linksland course.

At one time sailors called the Sankaty Head Light the "Blazing Star." Its only rival in magnificence was the twin towers at the highlands of the Navesink in New Jersey, the first to be outfitted with a Fresnel.

Courtesy of U.S. Coast Guard

Cape Florida Light

Most every follower of lighthouse lore knows the story of assistant keeper John Thompson's near-death plight against the Seminoles in 1836. You can read about it in virtually every lighthouse book that's ever been written.

But here's a Cape Florida story you've never heard before.

In May of 1992, my good friend William was returning from a business trip in the Key Biscayne area. While there, he visited the famed lighthouse. In the parking lot of Bill Baggs State Recreational Area, wherein the lighthouse is located, Will, a dour Scot, uncharacteristically pulled a hard-earned hundred dollar bill out of his wallet and took it with him.

He enjoyed the lighthouse tour and, afterward, entered a small grotto adjacent to the lighthouse where a monument stood. A brick walkway leading to the monument was being built, one brick at a time, by donations to the Cape Florida "Save Our Lighthouse" campaign. Each brick was inscribed with a person's name who had contributed $100 to the lighthouse preservation project. Will thought it might make the perfect $100 souvenir: it was better than any trinket. While considering it, he noticed a young woman seated inside the grotto. Beside her, playing quietly, was a young child. She turned her head slightly toward the man.

"One day I'm going to buy one of those bricks," the woman said hesitantly. "You see, the city of Miami just dedicated a coconut palm tree here today in memory of my brother, Alcides Vasquez."

Will looked past her to a tiny baby palm being watered by a park groundskeeper.

"He was murdered not long ago," she continued, lowering her head. "I would like to thank the park and the city by buying a brick in his honor, but..." her voice trailed off.

My friend now focused his full attention on the pretty señora. She began talking about her brother, a former park ranger at Bill Baggs — how his big heart, his positive outlook, and his generous ways were always available to others. Not three weeks before, Al Vasquez Jr. had been slain by semi-strangers. Al had opened up his home to these people when they found themselves in a jam. They reciprocated his kindness by killing him.

Will was stunned by the story and could say nothing. The woman began to cry gently.

Suddenly the man put it all together. He was meant to be there, at this precise time, for a particular purpose.

Without a word, Will put his hand into his pocket and withdrew the $100 bill. Placing it in the woman's hands, he said, "Your brother shall have his brick."

The woman was aghast. "No, no! I couldn't take that from you." She stammered, " I...I...what is your name? I don't even know you!"

Will had been taught long ago that if you truly wish to give a gift to someone, make it in such a way that it is impossible for them to repay you.

"It doesn't matter," he quietly reassured her. Then he left.

The groundskeeper, who had observed the moment between the two strangers, called out to Al Vasquez's sister after the man had gone.

"You see," he politely chided her, "there are some good people in this world."

Seven years later, Will was thinking about the touching exchange he had experienced with the woman that late spring Sunday afternoon at Cape Florida. On impulse, he called the lighthouse main office and asked if a brick dedicated to Al Vasquez had ever been donated to the lighthouse project.

After a short wait, a reply came from the other end. "Yes, there is a brick out there. It reads 'In loving memory of Al Vasquez Jr.'"

If you're ever down Key Biscayne way, you might check out the little coconut palm tree and the inscribed brick in memory of an unsung hero of humanity. And remember the quiet but important story of human love between two strangers, under the twilight shadows of the Cape Florida Lighthouse itself, that helped to perpetuate Al Vasquez's legacy of love.

Cindy Horovitz Wilson

Block Island (RI) Southeast Light

When my mother celebrated her 90th birthday, we reminisced about some of the many fun moments we've shared. One that wasn't so funny at the time, she says, was when we were on Block Island in the mid-1950s. One night we all went out to visit the magnificent Southeast Light.

I remember the octagonal red-brick tower, with its gleaming first-order green beam soaring more than 200 feet above the Atlantic, and the adjoining gothic-style two-family dwelling. I also recall a strange, almost yearning; a pulling by the edges of the massive rock bluff that we stood on.

"Yes, you wanted to jump," my mother said. "It frightened the heck out of me."

But what I have since learned is that having the push/pull sensation atop a cliff or tall building is not all that uncommon. Being at that great light that night is the kind of experience that as an adult you say, "I wish I'd paid better attention at the time." But then, a lot escapes the attention of a 10-year-old.

In 1993, the Southeast Light was pardoned from erosion by Block Island residents, who coughed up $2 million to relocate the lighthouse 245 feet inland.

Courtesy of U.S. Coast Guard

The Little Red Lighthouse

Little Brother, where is your light?
— Hildegarde Hoyt Swift
author,
The Little Red Lighthouse and the Great Gray Bridge

Not many people know it as Jeffries Hook Lighthouse. Most have always referred to it as the Little Red Lighthouse under the George Washington Bridge.

In fact, one of the most popular children's books of all time, *The Little Red Lighthouse and the Great Gray Bridge*, whose story line deals with the involuntary retirement of the Little Red Lighthouse when the gargantuan bridge is constructed, created such a stir upon publication that the Coast Guard offered the light, in 1951, to New York City's Parks Department.

The little, red, conical, steel-plated lighthouse lives up to its name. Just 40 feet high with a focal point (from beam to water) of 61 feet, it had served since 1920 as the first lighthouse that travelers encountered going up the Hudson River. Previous to that, two red stake lights had been in service since 1889. The little light warned mariners of the dangerous shoals off 178th Street until 1931, when the huge, monolithic George Washington Bridge no longer made the Little Red Lighthouse necessary.

Other Unforgettable Lighthouses

Admiralty Head (WA, 1903)
Assateague Island (VA/MD, 1833)
Barnegat (NJ, 1835)
Block Island North Light (RI, 1829)
Boston Light (MA, 1716)
Cape Flattery (WA, 1858)
Cape Lookout (NC, 1812)
Cape Neddick (ME, 1879)
Cape St. Elias (AK, 1916)
Cape St. George (FL, 1833)
Cleveland Light Station (OH, 1829)
Drum Point (MD, 1883)
Dunkirk (NY, 1829)
East Brother Island (CA, 1874)
Ft. Tompkins (NY, 1828)
Head Harbour (New Brunswick, Canada, 1829)
Heceta Head (OR, 1894)
Jupiter Inlet (FL, 1860)
Langara Point (British Columbia, 1913)
Makapuu Point (HI, 1909)
Mukilteo (WA, 1906)
Navesink Twin Lights (NJ, 1828)
Nayatt Point (RI, 1828)
North Head (WA, 1898)
Okracoke Island (NC, 1803)
Old Discovery Island (British Columbia, 1886)
Old Mackinac Point (MI, 1892)

Old Port Boca Grande (FL, 1890)
Old Presque Isle (MI, 1840)
Owls Head (ME, 1826)
Pemaquid Point (ME, 1827)
Pigeon Point (CA, 1872)
Pilot Island (WI, 1850)
Point Fermin (CA, 1874)
Point Pinos (CA, 1855)
Round Island (MI, 1895)
St. Simons (GA, 1810)
Sandy Hook (NJ, 1764)
Sentinel Island (AK, 1902)
Thatcher's Island Twin Lights (MA, 1771)
Thomas Point (MD, 1825)
Three Sisters of Nauset (MA, 1838)
Toledo Harbor (OH, 1904)
Yaquina Head (OR, 1873)

In 1934, a storm
of all storms hit and
threw twenty-foot waves
breaking onto the beach
and carried logs all the
way to U.S. Highway 1.
It was spooky, and some
of us thought it was
the end of the world.

Herman Jaehne
lighthouse child,
Pigeon Point Light (CA)

Chapter 12

The Keeper's Closet

First Lighthouse in U.S.
    Boston Light, Little Brewster Island, MA (1716)

First Screw-Pile Lighthouse in U.S.
    Brandywine Shoal, Delaware Bay (1850)

Tallest U.S. Lighthouse
    Cape Hatteras, North Carolina — 193 feet

Oldest U.S. Lighthouse
    Sandy Hook Light, New Jersey (1764)

First U.S. Lighthouse with a Fresnel Lens
    Navesink Twin Lights (NJ), 1840

Last Lighthouse Built in the U.S.
    Charleston, S.C., 1960

Tallest Lighthouse in the World
    Yokohama, Japan — 348-foot tower

Nearly 1,500 lighthouses were built in the United States. Less than 500 are now operating.

The Three Sisters of Nauset

One of the odd offshoots of the notorious Stephen Pleasonton reign as chief lighthouse administrator was the erection, in 1838, of the Three Sisters of Nauset: three 30-foot lighthouses that dotted the beaches at Nauset on Cape Cod, separated from one another by just 150 feet. They would become lighthouse history's only triple-light set.

In the period preceding flashing and occulting optics (1850), the unusual multiple string of lights was justified because coastal mariners needed to differentiate Nauset from Highland Light's single light to the north and the double lights of Chatham to the south.

The black-capped, squat towers from a distance could easily be mistaken for three ladies in white dresses and black bonnets, thus the origin of the name.

The quirky, one-of-a-kind configuration was an example of lighthouse largesse before technology improved and the cost-cutting measures of the Lighthouse Board took hold.

The sisters, at one time separated and sold as beach cottages to private owners, have been repurchased by the Cape Cod National Seashore for historical restoration and public display.

Haven't the Foggiest

Rhode Island's Beavertail Light, the third lighthouse built in the United States, has been the developing grounds for most of the advancements made in fog signal technology.

A firing cannon was first used at Boston Light, but Beavertail developed the fog bell and, most sensationally, Celadon Daboll's flared trumpets. One of the colorful by-products of the trumpet era was the invention, in 1852 at Beavertail, of a horse-powered pump used to create air pressure. Steam whistles, hot-air steam-engine-driven signals, and compressed air sirens also were tested there.

Though I'm sure you'd have an argument from the keepers of Point Reyes Light off San Francisco and any number of other West Coast lighthouses, it is Maine's Seguin Island that holds the record as the foggiest location in America. One year its fog signal logged an incredible 2,734 hours of use.

Florida's Lights Required New Approach

In the 1820s, lighthouses began to be built along the Florida coastline, but from the outset they posed unique problems for engineers in their construction.

The traditional New England, brick-based tower was not suited for most of the sites where lighthouses were planned in Florida, particularly in the Florida Keys, where some structures had to be built offshore in the water itself. The weight of the giant conical towers so common up north would create foundational problems in the soft, sand-based land of Florida's shores.

It was with these constraints in mind that, ultimately, the screw-pile lighthouse was born — spindly, skeletal frameworks that used huge iron spikes or "piles" with screw-type blades on the tips to "screw" into the deep sand and coral rock bottoms below the sea's sand and dirt level. These lighthouses, beginning with the rebuilt Carysfort Light in 1852, offered little resistance to high hurricane winds that, from time to time, battered the southern shores of the United States. The keepers' quarters were usually located on an enclosed platform within the framework about 20 or thirty feet above the sea.

The Pensacola Light, a brick tower lit in 1825, was the first lighthouse built in Florida.

Superior Desolation

Lake Superior's Stannard Rock Light, a desolate outpost on a mile-long reef that rises slightly above the water level at its northern end, occasionally entombed its keepers when violent wave-action froze on the outside of the tower. The site was instantly viewed as a threat to navigation when first discovered by Captain Charles C. Stannard, in 1835, and the Lighthouse Board, in its 1866 report, called it "the most serious danger to navigation in Lake Superior." For 80 years it was a "stag" station, a lighthouse that only men inhabited, because it was believed to be too severe a way of life for women or families. In light of that, Stannard Rock Light has been dubiously nicknamed "The Loneliest Place in the World."

It's like trying to navigate in a wheat field.

Anonymous sea captain
after navigating down the length of the
St. Lawrence Seaway, with its low headlands
and few distinctive shoreline features

Over this bare Highland the wind has full sweep. Even in July it blows the wings over the heads of young turkeys, which do not know enough to head against it;…and you must hold onto the lighthouse to prevent being blown into the Atlantic.

Henry David Thoreau
on the Highland (Cape Cod) Light

It has been very cold here for the last Month and the most ice I ever see in this Rigen We are almost buried up in it. No salt water to be seen from the Island i have not seen a Living man for over a month no prospect for the better I do get the blues sometimes

Herman Dill
keeper, Billingsgate Island Light,
February 7, 1875

Keep the Light Burning

*It's a thrill to carry on the tradition of all
the Lighthouse Service and Coast Guard
keepers who have been here before me. I
don't think I'm going to get the full impact
of it all until I leave here and look back
and say, "Wow, that was a pretty neat job."*
— Scott Stanton
*U.S. Coast Guard petty officer
and one of three men on duty at Boston Light —
the first, and last, manned lighthouse
in the United States*

The Boston Light on Little Brewster Island, at
the mouth of the entrance to Boston's harbor, generally recognized as America's first lighthouse
(1716), is also the last manned lighthouse in the
United States. As a gesture of respect to the age-
old institution of lighthouse keepers and the invalu-
able service that they rendered, the U.S. Coast
Guard continues to assign a three-man staff to carry
out the maintenance duties at the historic tower. It
is considered an honor to draw the assignment.

Sea Dog Receives Full Seaman's Burial

Sport, the longtime canine companion of the lighthouse tender *Hyacinth*, began his legacy with the ship from the moment he was pulled aboard as a bedraggled and scrawny spotted mongrel during a thunderstorm on the Milwaukee River in 1914. For the next 12 years the dog would be a friend to all on the ship's supply voyages to lighthouses along Lake Michigan.

Considered a regular member of the crew, he joined the men in swimming, baseball games, and excursions ashore. Eventually Sport gained longer tenure on the *Hyacinth* than any officer or crewman during that span.

The likeable sea dog died of old age on July 19, 1926, and, with all hands mustered on the spar deck, was given a full seaman's salute upon a freshwater bier, buried in the same sea from which he was rescued a dozen years before.

More Santa

Gifts were often extended to the keepers by caring citizens of lighthouse area communities. The government frowned on such practices, but the citizenry gave from its collective heart anyway. As would be expected, the gifts were warmly welcomed by the lighthouse keepers and their families.

A number of southern New England keepers were given radios annually by a benevolent donor, Mrs. Edward Harkness of Waterford, Connecticut. It was generally known that she had a special appreciation for lighthouses and the families that tended them.

Ribbon candy, dispensed to the keepers at the Harbor of Refuge light in Delaware Bay every Christmas, usually arrived in a million smashed little pieces, while the crew at the New London Ledge Light received gifts that included books and magazines from the local women's club.

Boaters would occasionally pass along a six-pack of beer, even though alcohol was verboten, and local fishermen offered their finest catch, including lobsters, to the men and families at the lights come holiday time.

Unusual History, Structures Mark Garden Key (Your Name Is Mud)

A year after Florida became a state (1845), the U.S. Corps of Engineers began erecting a monstrous fortress on tiny Garden Key in the Dry Tortugas, the Gateway to the Gulf, 70 miles west beyond land's end of the Florida Keys. Government officials recognized that a military presence on the easternmost islet of the two 'Tugas (Loggerhead Key is the other) would mean supremacy of the Gulf and control of navigation to the fertile Mississippi Valley.

For the next 30 years, the mammoth garrison known as Fort Jefferson would be constructed on the little 567-yard spit of sand, using more than 40 million bricks and buttressed by eight-foot-thick walls. Still, the huge project was never completed.

The original Dry Tortugas Lighthouse, built in 1825, was later resituated atop the battlements of the fort and became a dependable harbor light.

A fascinating footnote in the assassination of Abraham Lincoln was written at Ft. Jefferson. Maryland physician Dr. Samuel Mudd was sentenced to life imprisonment there for having set the broken leg of Lincoln assassin John Wilkes Booth. Though later pardoned after valiantly battling the ravaging yellow fever epidemic at the fort in 1867, Mudd's unfortunate plight would spawn the well-known phrase, "Your name is Mud."

I had a classmate who fitted for college by the lamps of a lighthouse, which was more light, we think, than the University afforded.

Henry David Thoreau

Bibliography
and Index

Bibliography

Bartlett, John. Familiar Quotations. Boston: Little, Brown & Company, 1855.

Bauman, Richard. "Beacons by the Sea." Catholic Digest. April 1995: 32, 34.

Clark, Admont G. Lighthouses of Cape Cod – Martha's Vineyard – Nantucket. Hyannis, MA: Parnassus Imprints, Inc. 1992.

Corbett, Christopher. "Maine Landings." The Washington Post. 1 August 1993, E1, E8-9.

Dean, Love. The Lighthouses of Hawaii. Honolulu: University of Hawaii Press, 1991.

De Wire, Elinor. Guide to Florida Lighthouses. Englewood, FL: Pineapple Press, Inc., 1987.

De Wire, Elinor. Guardians of the Lights. Sarasota, FL: Pineapple Press, Inc. 1995.

Evans, Bergen. Dictionary of Quotations. New York: Delacorte Press, 1968.

Fleming, Candace. Women of the Lights. Morton Grove, IL: Albert Whitman & Company, 1996.

Gibbons, Gail. Beacons of Light – Lighthouses. New York: William Morrow & Company, Inc., 1990.

Gibbs, Jim A. Lighthouses of the Pacific. West Chester, PA: Schiffer Publishing Ltd., 1986.

Gifford, Mary Louise and J. Candace Gifford. Women Who Kept the Lights. Williamsburg, VA: Cypress Communications, 1993.

Grant, John and Ray Jones. Legendary Lighthouses. Old Saybrook, CT: The Globe Pequot Press, 1998.

Hart, James D. Oxford Companion to American Literature. 4th Edition. New York: Oxford University Press, 1965.

Holland, F. Ross, Jr. Great American Lighthouses. Washington, D.C.: The Preservation Press, 1989.

Holland, F. Ross, Jr. America's Lighthouses – An Illustrated History. New York: Dover Publications, Inc., 1988.

Hyde, Charles K. The Northern Lights. Lansing, MI: TwoPeninsula Press, 1986.

Langdon-Jones, Commander R., R.N. Silent Sentinels. London: Frederick Muller, Ltd. 1944.

Lighthouses of New England. Videotape. Prod. Susan Sulavik Peters. Connecticut Public Television, 1988.

Mathan, Christiane and William D. Barry. "Portland Head." The Keeper's Log. Vol.VII, No. 4. San Francisco: U.S. Lighthouse

Society, Summer 1991: 4.

McCarthy, Kevin M. Florida Lighthouses. Gainesville, FL: University of Florida Press, 1990.

McCormick, W.H. The Modern Book of Lighthouses. London: A.&C. Black, Ltd., 1936.

Michelet, Jules. The Sea. London, Edinburgh & New York: T. Nelson & Sons, 1875.

Morris, Gerald E., ed. The Log of Mystic Seaport. Vol. 31, No. 1. Mystic, CT, Spring 1979.

Noble, Dennis L. Lighthouses & Keepers. Annapolis, MD: Naval Institute Press, 1997.

Oxford Dictionary of Quotations. 3rd Edition. New York: Oxford University Press, 1979.

Radzak, Lee. "Split Rock." The Keeper's Log. Vol. VII, No. 1. San Francisco: U.S. Lighthouse Society, 1990: 2-7.

Roberts, Bruce and Ray Jones. Great Lakes Lighthouses. Old Saybrook, CT: The Globe Pequot Press, 1994.

Roberts, Bruce and Ray Jones. Southern Lighthouses. Chester, CT: Globe Pequot Press, 1989.

Shelton-Roberts, Cheryl and Bruce Roberts. Lighthouse Families. Birmingham, AL: Crane Hill Publishers, 1997.

Snow, Edward Rowe. Famous Lighthouses of America. New York: Dodd, Mead & Company, 1955.

Snow, Edward Rowe. The Lighthouses of New England. New York: Dodd, Mead & Company, 1973.

Stephens, David E. Lighthouses of Nova Scotia. Windsor, Nova Scotia: Lancelot Press, 1973.

Sterling, Robert Thayer. Lighthouses of the Maine Coast and the Men Who Keep Them. Brattleboro, VT: Stephen Daye Press, 1935.

Swift, Hildegarde H. and Lynd Ward. The Little Red Lighthouse and the Great Gray Bridge. San Diego, London, New York: Harcourt Brace Jovanovich Publishers, 1942.

Welch, Wally. The Lighthouses of Maine. Apopka, FL: Lighthouse Publications, 1990.

Welch, Wally. The Lighthouses of Massachusetts. Apopka, FL: Lighthouse Publications, 1989.

Welch, Wally. The Lighthouses of Rhode Island. Apopka, FL: Lighthouse Publications, 1987.

Witney, Dudley. The Lighthouse. Boston: New York Graphic Society, 1975.

Wright, Larry & Patricia. Bonfires & Beacons: Great Lakes Lighthouses. Erin, Ontario: Boston Mills Press, 1996.

Index

Index

About the Author

Alan Ross is a writer and sports historian living with his wife, Karol, in Monteagle, Tennessee. A graduate of Fordham University, he is a former editor for Professional Team Publications, Athlon Sports Communications, and Walnut Grove Press. His feature articles on sports history have appeared in *The Sporting News*, *Lindy's*, *Athlon Sports*, *Athletic Administration*, *Game Day*, *NFL Insider*, *Arizona Cardinals Media Guide*, *The Coffin Corner*, and *Track Record*. He is also the history columnist for *Titans Exclusive*, the official publication of the NFL's Tennessee Titans. Ross has written seven books on sports for Walnut Grove Press. *The Lure of Lighthouses* is his second non-sports book.

For information about books from Walnut Grove Press, call 1-800-256-8584.